A GREAT DAY FOR
SNORKELING

by Nuria Martín

illustrated by
Cathy Diefendorf

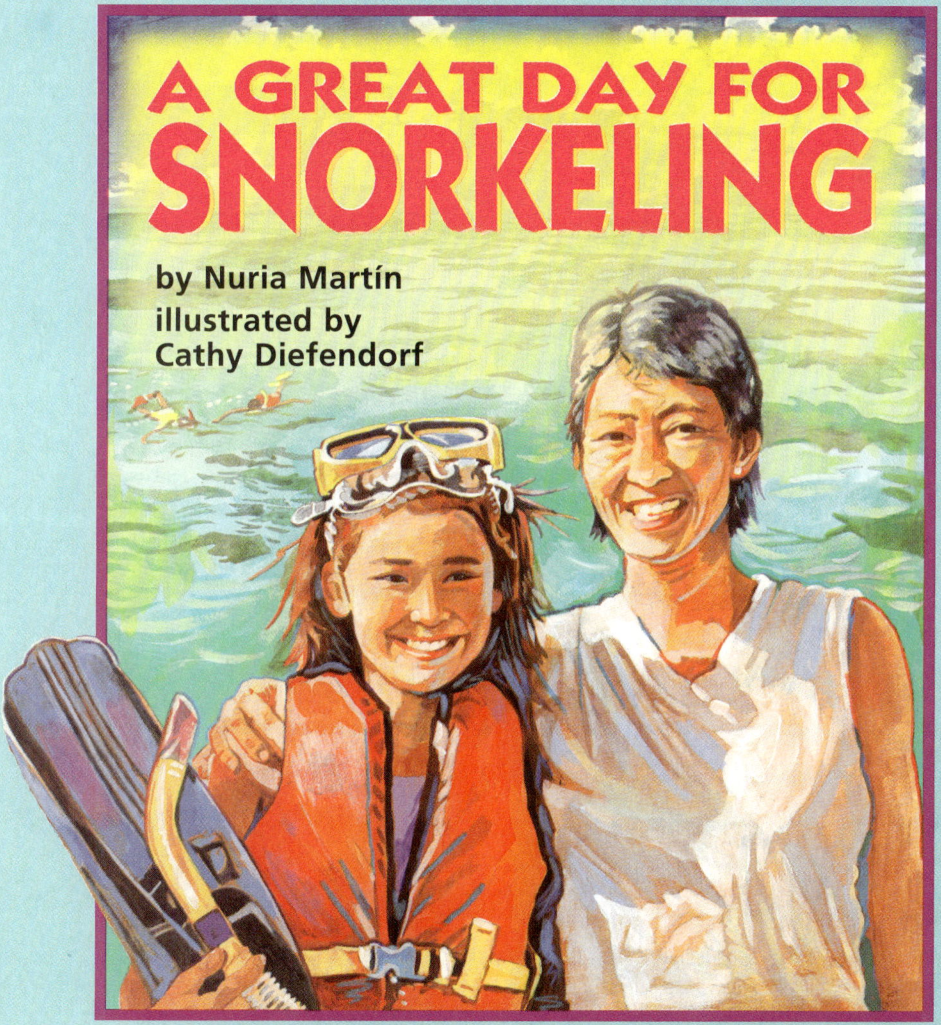

HOUGHTON MIFFLIN   BOSTON

"It's a great day for snorkeling," I said.
"It's a great day for a boat ride," said Grandma.

"Grandma, you'll love snorkeling," I said.
She was afraid to try it. I could tell.

"Snorkeling sounds like something pigs do!" she said. "I'll just stay on the boat and read."

"But you said you'd try!" I told her.
"I guess I changed my mind," she said.

The boat stopped. I pulled on my mask.
"I'm going in without you," I said.

The water looked deep and dark.
But I jumped right in.

The water felt warm as a hug. I saw
colorful fish all around.

Suddenly there was a big splash.
The water got cloudy. I saw only bubbles.

A dark shape was moving closer. My
heart pounded fast. Was it a shark?

I popped my head out of the water.
"Grandma!" I shouted back at the boat.

But she wasn't there! I started paddling
fast. Something grabbed my leg!

"Grandma, help!" I yelled again.
"Here I am!" said a voice next to me.

It was Grandma!

"I thought you were a shark," I said.

"That's because I swim like a fish," said Grandma.

"I thought snorkeling was for pigs!" I said.
"I guess I changed my mind," she said. We
both laughed. Then we dove back under.

Grandma pointed at the blue and yellow fish.
I could tell what she was thinking.
"What a great day for snorkeling!"